• WEIRD SCIENCE •

MILITARY

HOW THE HECK DOES THAT WORK ?!

VIRGINIA LOH-HAGAN

45TH PARALLEL PRESS

Published in the United States of America by Cherry Lake Publishing Group
Ann Arbor, Michigan
www.cherrylakepublishing.com

Reading Adviser: Beth Walker Gambro, MS, Ed., Reading Consultant, Yorkville, IL
Book Designer: Felicia Macheske

45th Parallel Press is an imprint of Cherry Lake Publishing Group.

Library of Congress Cataloging-in-Publication Data

Names: Loh-Hagan, Virginia, author.
Title: Weird science: military / by Virginia Loh-Hagan.
Description: Ann Arbor, Michigan : Cherry Lake Publishing, [2021]
  | Series: How the heck does that work?! | Includes index.
Identifiers: LCCN 2021004904 (print) | LCCN 2021004905 (ebook)
  | ISBN 9781534187641 (hardcover) | ISBN 9781534189041 (paperback)
  | ISBN 9781534190443 (pdf) | ISBN 9781534191846 (ebook)
Subjects: LCSH: United States—Armed Forces—Juvenile literature. |
  Military art and science. | Warships—United States--Juvenile
  literature. | Chemical warfare—Juvenile literature. |
  Parachuting—United States—Juvenile literature.
Classification: LCC UA23 .L656 2021 (print) | LCC UA23 (ebook) | DDC
  623—dc23
LC record available at https://lccn.loc.gov/2021004904
LC ebook record available at https://lccn.loc.gov/2021004905

Cherry Lake Publishing Group would like to acknowledge the work of the Partnership for 21st Century Learning,
a Network of Battelle for Kids. Please visit *http://www.battelleforkids.org/networks/p21* for more information.

Printed in the United States of America
Corporate Graphics

**Dr. Virginia Loh-Hagan is an author, university professor, and former classroom teacher.
She's currently the Director of the Asian Pacific Islander Desi American Resource Center at
San Diego State University. She lives near several military bases. She lives in San Diego
with her very tall husband and very naughty dogs.**

TABLE OF CONTENTS

The president of the United States is the commander in chief. This person controls the military.

INTRODUCTION

All kinds of weird science happen in the military. The military is our fighting force. They protect our security. They protect our way of life. The U.S. Armed Forces includes the Air Force, Army, Coast Guard, Marine Corps, Navy, and Space Force.

There are 3 types of military workers. Some are on active duty. This includes soldiers and sailors. Others are in the **reserve**. This means they're on call. They serve when needed. The rest are **veterans**. Veterans are military members who have retired or left the military.

The military needs people for all kinds of jobs. Some people fight in battle. Some people fly planes. Some people work on ships. Some people serve as officers. Some people cook and clean. All jobs are important.

The military also has scientists. Military scientists invent new weapons. They invent new tools and gear. They study warfare. They improve fighting strategies. They improve training practices. They use technology. They receive **intelligence**. Intelligence means information.

Many soldiers get hurt in war. They need care. The military has hospitals to treat injured soldiers. They want to protect soldiers. They find new ways to improve soldiers' health.

Dare to learn more about military science! So much is going on. How the heck does it all work?

The U.S. military has bases in more than 70 countries.

Campers eat MREs as well. MREs are also given to help feed poor communities.

CHAPTER 1

MREs

What was the last thing you ate? In war, food is not always available. Soldiers eat MREs. MRE stands for "Meals, Ready to Eat." MREs are packed foods. They're **portioned** for individual soldiers. Portions are sizes.

U.S. Navy SEALs are special forces. SEALs stands for "Sea, Air, and Land Forces" They work in extreme conditions. They carry heavy loads on foot. They serve on long missions. MREs are light and flat. They're easy to carry. They don't need to be cooked. But they can be heated up. MREs also include a flameless heater. MREs can be eaten on the go. MREs are good for 3 years.

Soldiers can choose from many MRE dishes. They include a main dish, side, dessert, snack, and powdered drink.

The flexible pouches mean the meals can be handled roughly.

Human bodies need energy to work. Scientists make sure MREs have enough **calories** and nutrients. Calories are units of energy. The scientists work to improve MREs. They make them healthier. They make them taste better and last longer. They create more choices.

The key to MREs is the pouch. It is made of thick foil. It has plastic layers. It's strong and flexible.

MRE pouches are filled with food. They're sealed tightly. They're boiled. This **sterilizes** what's inside. Sterilize means to clean and keep free of germs. The pouches are flat. This shape takes less time to heat. It also makes the food taste better.

Carriers launch an aircraft every 25 seconds.

CHAPTER 2

AIRCRAFT CARRIERS

Have you ever seen an aircraft carrier? Aircraft carriers are warships. They're moving military bases. They carry planes and jets. They're huge. Carriers have short **runways**. Runways are strips of land for aircraft to take off and land.

Aircraft need a boost when taking off on a carrier. This is because runways on carriers are too short. Without a boost, these aircraft will fall into the ocean. Carriers have **catapults**. Catapults are launching tools. They store and then release energy. This energy changes into motion.

Front wheels of planes are hooked to catapults. Catapults shoot the aircraft into the air. They transfer their energy to the aircraft. They go 150 miles (241 kilometers) per hour. This happens in 2 seconds. Aircraft are launched. Then, catapults are pulled back. The next aircraft is hooked up.

Even WEIRDER MILITARY SCIENCE!

- Aviator means pilot. Aviator sunglasses are popular today. But they were designed for pilots. Pilots used to wear goggles. But they couldn't see well with them at high altitudes. Altitude means height above ground. Aviator sunglasses were invented. They're light. They have green lenses. The lenses improved vision.

- Soldiers have served for years in Iraq and Afghanistan. Bombs called improvised explosive devices (IEDs) often injured soldiers. They hit them below the waist. Because of this, a company worked on creating special underwear. The underwear would protect soldiers' private parts. In 2010, this company made "Blast Boxers." This underwear was designed to be bomb-proof. They used Kevlar. Kevlar is used in many things including bulletproof vests. After seeing this, the U.S. Army started to work on its own product. It's called the "Pelvic Protection System."

- Autopsies are examinations of dead bodies. Everyone in the military who dies while on duty gets an autopsy. Even military dogs get one. Scientists study the bodies. They want to find new treatments. They want to create new tools. They want to help those injured in wars.

Landing an aircraft on a carrier is even harder. Pilots need to land at the right angle. A lighting system was created to help. This system helps guide pilots. It lets pilots know if they're in the correct place.

To land on a carrier, pilots fly over the runway. The crew then lays out several wires for the aircraft's **tailhook**. Tailhooks are at the end of aircraft. Tailhooks catch a wire. The wires slow the aircraft to a stop. The wires make sure aircrafts don't run off the carrier. The wires are attached to tubes. These tubes are below deck. A special mechanical system, called an arresting gear, takes in the aircraft's energy. This stops the aircraft.

Some pilots miss the wires when landing.
They fly off the carrier. They try again.

Submarines are also used to study the oceans.

CHAPTER 3

SUBMARINES

Can you imagine living underwater? **Submarines** are underwater warships. They patrol oceans. They find enemies. They fire missiles underwater. They can stay underwater for several months. They can **propel** themselves underwater. Propel means to move or push forward.

People can't live underwater. There's no air to breathe. There's a lot of water pressure. But they can live in submarines. Submarines are designed to protect people. They have 2 steel **hulls**. A hull is a sub or ship's body. The outer hull keeps water out. The inner hull is called the pressure hull. It's strong. It resists water pressure.

There's space between the 2 hulls. It holds tanks filled with air or water. These tanks are used as **ballast**. Ballast is heavy material used to make ships stable. When the ballast tanks are full of air, submarines rise to the surface. When filled with water, submarines sink deeper into the ocean.

Some submarines have nuclear engines. Nuclear power is created by splitting atoms. Atoms are the smallest part of all elements. These engines provide heat. They make electricity that powers all the sub's systems. Submarines make their own oxygen. They separate oxygen molecules from water. They make their own drinking water. They use electricity to remove salt from seawater.

Trash is crushed into steel cans. It's released from a watertight exit. It's dumped on the ocean floor.

UNSOLVED MYSTERY

The USS *Cyclops* was a large ship. It carried materials needed to make weapons. It had a crew of more than 300 people. In 1918, it crossed the Bermuda Triangle. This area of the Atlantic Ocean is between Florida, Bermuda, and Puerto Rico. The ship disappeared. No trace of it was ever found. It set a record in U.S. Naval history. It's the largest loss of life not caused by war. In 1945, 5 Navy planes flew over the Bermuda Triangle. They were on a training mission called Flight 19. Their compasses stopped working. A compass is a tool that helps pilots find places. The planes flew the wrong way during a storm. There were 14 airmen on the planes. The planes and the airmen were never seen again. People wonder about the area. They call it the "deadly Bermuda Triangle." Many people, planes, and boats get lost in this area. About 20 boats and 4 planes are lost per year. No one knows exactly why.

The U.S. military trains dolphins
at a base in San Diego, California.

CHAPTER 4

MILITARY DOLPHINS

Did you know the military trains dolphins? The military works with bottlenose dolphins. These dolphins rescue lost swimmers. They find submarines and enemy ships. They push warning buttons. They guard nuclear weapons. They find deep sea **mines**. Mines are bombs.

Dolphins are one of the world's smartest animals. They can communicate. They send messages in different ways. They squeak. They leap. They slap their tails. They blow bubbles. They have special whistles. They click. These clicks are high-pitched sounds. They're used for **echolocation**. Echolocation is using sound waves to find things.

TEST IT OUT!

The military relies on its planes. Planes fight in the skies. They deliver supplies. They transport soldiers. The design of planes affects how they work. Forces act on planes so they can fly. Forces push or pull. Learn more about planes.

Materials

- Instructions on how to make a paper airplane
- Paper
- Paper clip

1. Look up instructions on how to make a paper airplane. Make the airplane. Throw it in the air. This pushes the plane forward. This force is called thrust.

2. Watch the plane fly forward. Air moves over and under the wings. This provides an upward lift force on the plane. Air also pushes back against the plane. This slows it down. This is a drag force. Drag is a force that resists air movement.

3. Add a paper clip to the paper plane. Throw it in the air again. Weight affects its flight. Gravity pulls it down toward Earth. Gravity is a force. It causes things to fall to Earth.

4. Change the plane's shape. See how much drag it experiences. Changing forces on the plane affects how well it flies.

The military uses dolphins for their echolocation skills. When a dolphin makes a clicking sound, the sound hits an object in the water. The sound bounces off the object and travels back to the dolphin. The sound comes back as an echo.

Echolocation gives dolphins a lot of information. It shows them the shape, size, speed, distance, and location of objects. This is how dolphins find things. Dolphins also have excellent hearing.

Trainers give dolphins things to find. Dolphins return those things. Trainers give fish or other rewards to the dolphins. Trainers take care of dolphins. They keep the dolphins healthy and fit.

The military uses other animals. They use horses, pigeons, and dogs.

Paratroopers wear warm clothes to avoid frostbite.

CHAPTER 5

MILITARY PARACHUTING

Have you ever been on a plane? Imagine jumping from it! The military trains soldiers to do this. Military planes fly in high altitudes. High altitudes can be dangerous. The air is thin. There's less oxygen. The air pressure is low. The air is also very cold. Our bodies use oxygen to keep warm. This means our lungs have to work really hard to breathe. We breathe faster and deeper. We have to take in more oxygen. Our hearts beat faster.

Soldiers who jump out of planes are called **paratroopers**. They have to do breathing exercises. They use oxygen bottles.

SCIENTIST SPOTLIGHT

Harshwardhansinh Zala is a teen inventor. He invented a drone that detects landmines. Landmines are small bombs. They explode when stepped on. About 110 million landmines are still active. They kill or hurt more than 5,000 people every year. Zala saw a video of soldiers looking for landmines. Soldiers put their lives at risk doing this. Zala wanted to help people safely find landmines. At age 15, he started a company. His drone flies over fields. It scans the ground. It sends real-time signals to the army base. It drops a package on the landmine. This sets off the landmine. There is no human risk. Zala's invention is called EAGLE A7. He built it with a 3-D printer. 3-D means three-dimensional. It means not looking flat. It was developed over 3 years. Zala plans to give his invention to his government.

Military planes fly above enemy skies. They fly in secret missions. They need to be quiet. They don't want to be seen. They drop off supplies. They drop off soldiers.

Paratroopers use **parachutes** to get safely to the ground. Parachutes are made of thin cloth. They're flexible for steering reasons. They're strong for safety reasons. They're lightweight and can be folded. They are easy to carry.

Parachutes are pulled down by gravity. But parachutes open up like umbrellas. Because of this, parachutes create drag. Parachutes slow a jumper's fall. This allows the jumper to land safely.

The military uses dome-shaped parachutes.

People wear protective gear to avoid biochemical warfare.

CHAPTER 6

CHEMICAL WARFARE

Have you ever had a skin rash? Your skin may have been in contact with a chemical. Your body reacted. It broke out.

The military uses chemical warfare. It is the use of chemicals as weapons. These chemicals are poisons. They're called **agents**. Agents are things that produce an effect. Agents cause reactions when in contact with humans.

Most agents start as **liquids**. Liquids are substances that flow like water. When used in war, agents are often turned into **gases**. Gases are substances that are like air and can spread quickly. During war, this is done with sprays or explosions.

Herbicides are used as weapons. They kill crops.
This destroys an enemy's food source.

There are different types of chemical agents. Nerve agents send signals to organs and muscles. They cause pain. Blister agents affect the eyes, lungs, skin, and stomach. They cause blisters and burns. Choking agents attack the lungs. Victims **suffocate**. Suffocate means being unable to breathe. Blood agents also cause victims to suffocate. But these agents are absorbed in the blood. They stop the body's ability to use oxygen.

VX is the most dangerous. It's a nerve agent. It doesn't smell or taste like anything. It's slow to die out. It stays on surfaces for days. In cold places, it can last for months. Even when exposed to a tiny amount of VX, people can experience sweating and muscle twitching. Other symptoms include watery eyes, coughing, headaches, and sometimes even death! There are treatments. However, they must be used quickly to work.

GLOSSARY

agents (AY-juhnts) things that cause reactions

ballast (BAL-uhst) heavy material used to make ships stable

calories (KAL-uh-rees) units of energy

catapults (KAT-uh-puhltz) devices that launch objects

echolocation (e-koh-loh-KAY-shuhn) the process of using sound waves to find things

gases (GAS-ess) substances that are like air

hulls (HUHLZ) bodies of ships or submarines

intelligence (in-TEL-uh-juhnss) information about the enemy

liquids (LIK-wids) substances that flow like water

mines (MINES) bombs that are set off when touched

parachutes (PA-ruh-shootz) devices made of thin, strong cloth used to slow a paratroopers' descents

paratroopers (PAR-uh-troo-puhrz) soldiers who jump out of planes

portioned (POR-shuhnd) sized for individual use

propel (pruh-PEL) to move or push forward

reserve (ri-ZURV) soldiers who are not active duty but are available to serve when needed

runways (RUHN-wayz) areas of land used by aircraft for taking off and landing

sterilizes (STER-uh-lizez) cleans in order to be free from germs

submarines (SUHB-muh-reens) underwater warships

suffocate (SUHF-uh-kate) to stop breathing

tailhook (TAYL-hook) an extended hook attached to an aircraft's tail

veterans (VET-ur-uhns) military members who have retired or left the military

LEARN MORE

Spears, James, and John Perritano. *Everything Battles: Arm Yourself with Fierce Photos and Fascinating Facts*. Washington, DC: National Geographic Kids, 2013.

Tank: The Definitive Visual History of Armored Vehicles. New York, NY: DK Publishing, 2017.

INDEX